Before The Apocalypse

To Maya

From

Before The Apocalypse

BUSTA

XULON PRESS

Xulon Press
2301 Lucien Way #415
Maitland, FL 32751
407.339.4217
www.xulonpress.com

© 2022 by Busta

All rights reserved solely by the author. The author guarantees all contents are original and do not infringe upon the legal rights of any other person or work. No part of this book may be reproduced in any form without the permission of the author.

Due to the changing nature of the Internet, if there are any web addresses, links, or URLs included in this manuscript, these may have been altered and may no longer be accessible. The views and opinions shared in this book belong solely to the author and do not necessarily reflect those of the publisher. The publisher therefore disclaims responsibility for the views or opinions expressed within the work.

Paperback ISBN-13: 978-1-66285-224-4
Ebook ISBN-13: 978-1-66285-225-1

Table Of Contents

1 Why Do Good People Do Bad Things 1
2 What Dreams A Christan Should Have And
   How To Make Them Come True. 19
3 The Reality Of Wars And Rumors Of War 29
4 Youtube Prophets 37
5 Prophet Or Mental Patient. 45
6 Prophecies And Suicide 55
7 Future Christans 69
8 Eternity In The Balance 79
9 In Memory Of The Fallen. 89
10 Mezmorized By The World 99
11 Held Captive By Religion. 109
12 Freedom In Christ 117

Introduction

Why do good people pretend to be bad. And bad people pretend to be good. ALSo why do good people do bad things. While bad people do good things.

These are just some of the questions i will be answering in this book. As well as what leads to these things. Also you will hear how to become a successful Christan in the worldy society we live in. And how to let your light shine for Christ.

I will discuss bible prophecy and current events. And the future of America and the church. As well as, what we will be doing in the millennial reign.

Chapter One

WHY DO GOOD PEOPLE DO BAD THINGS

From the beginning of time.
Man and women have worn a mask to
Cover up their Shame. From adam and eve
in the garden. To the Kings of the
earth and its princes. Hiding from
the face of god, In revelations.

Fear of God and man is the reason.
A fear of man is the reason why Good
People pretend to be bad. They are aware
that being an uprighT man in today's
Society can make you a target for
Ungodly people, to take advantage of
you.

In many cases christans in
Society, are the public's wiping board.
Many people are against Christ.
Because they dont want to Live their
lives according to the biblical Standards
set for them. So they use any excuse
they can to Justify their ungodly
beHavior.

They say things like the bible has
been tampered with. All Christans
are hypocrites. Priest are child molesters.
Anything they can conjure up to
Justify their ungodly behavior they
will.

When society see's a christan
living the victorious christan life,
It threatens their ideology.
It Shows them that the word of
God is true. And that it can be lived

they start to develop a fear, that
they will have to answer to God for
their ungodly lifestyle. Instead of
turning away from their sins. They
would rather mock and scoff at GoDly
people.

When a man or women of god encounters
this kind of Criticism. they can Do
Only two things. TAke the burden upon
themselves or lay it at the feet of
Christ. Sometimes upright
Christans fall short and take the
Criticism personally, and bear this
burden upon themselVEs

I was one of those people

This is why some good people
act bad. IT's because they see
that, no matter How upright a man
or women is. Their will always be
negative Criticism about his or her
person. No matter how one Strives
foR perfection. Their will always
be people that would like to
drag you down.

Many times what happens is,
we puT on the mask. And respond
to their criticism with our own
Criticism. And we start to
question the very faith that has
been our foundation.

We sometimes think to
Ourselves. Here i am feeding the poor
Preaching God's word and these same
People i'm trying to help are mocking
and scoffing at me.
                                      Justice in
Where is the Justice in this?

We begin to question God, as into why He would allow these
things to occur. We allow these
Situations to make us bitter.

The enemy see's our weakness
and starts to Lead us into a
negative mind state. He begins to play
off of our emotions.

A man or woman of god.
That falls from grace like this.
Can at times be more Dangerous
than an immoral ungodly person.

This brings us into the next
Question. Why do good people do bad
things.

When the foundation of a mans
Intellect and Heart are Suddenly
Changed or challenged. A mans
nature and mental Stability are in
Jeopardy. It Could easily cause a
mental breakdown. Right and
Wrong are no longer the guiding
Principles of that person's life.

The good that a man once did
could now be consiDered his moral
enemy. A Christan Who was once
the pillar in his community is no
longer. His Acts of kindness are now

Believed by Him to be the
enemy of His life, and the
Cause of His Heartache.

A man who once Knew to do good. Now does evil.

Lucifer is a good example of
what happens when a good being
foes bad.

A man or women who falls from
grace can be very dangerous
because the good they did for ChrisT
is no Longer the driving force of
their lives.

Unbelievers are immoral
because they are selfish and
ignorant. But a christan that
turns immoral, Does so with
a personal grudge against the
Lord and his Creation. They
act out in ways far more Destructive
than those who are JuST blind
and ignorant. to the truth.

Let's Look at Lucifer Isaiah 14 (13-14)
I Will Ascend to the heavens. I will raise my
thrown above the stars of God.
I will siT enthroned on the
mount of Assembly. I will Ascend
Above the tops of the Clouds.
I will make myself like the most
high.

Most immoral people would
not dare to say they will make
themselves greater than god.
Even though they may act like
it. But a Christan with a personal
Van Detta against god. Who Knows
Gods ways, will act in a malicious
way towards God and life.

They realize what they do is
Wrong. As Did Lucifer and they
they will be held accountable for
their wrongs. So they exercise
Vengeance against God and their
enemies Knowing their time
is short. They will steal kill
and Destroy until they get
What they want.

Many times they will
Literally sell their souls for
earthly gain. These are the
most dangerous people. Their
names are great in society
from rappers to Actors, From
rock stars to pornstars. Even
Preachers.

Mental illness can cause
Godly and ungodly people To do terrible
things. Mental illness can come
from a crack in the foundation
If ones mind.From physical
deficiency or from stress and
unforgiveness.

I personally suffer from a illness
Known as schizoaffective Disorder

A man or women who suffers
from this Disorder. And also has,
deep rooted Christan beliefs can
easily become a religious extremist.

A man acting in a religious
manner. Who also has a schizophrenic
tic or schizoaffective disorder. May
act irrationally. And because of his
religious beliefs he may Justify his
behavior. With the word of god.
Untreated this is a recipe for
Disaster. And the person suffering
from this DisorDer. May become a
Victim or victimize others.

I have spent a lot of time under
both religious princiPles and worldly
iDeology. I have AlSo spent a lot
of time entertaining an unHealthy
obsession with endtime events and
Prophesy. I believe for a long time
that the end was near.

Now i'm not saying that
endtime Prophecy is a crazy
or irrational thought. But to be
So obsessed with it, to the
piont where you are not wanting to
Live your life. Is very Destructive
to one's personal life. And the
Lives of others.

We must remember that Jesus
told us to occupy until
the end.

Sometimes we as believers
rush ahead of the Lord.
And focus on the end instead
of the beginning. The curse instead of the blessing.

To focus on the problem
instead of the solution. Can often
Lead us into a mental and physical
breakDown. The cosT of War
Casting our cares at the feet of
Jesus, Can be Devastating

At one piont in my life it
Cost me my freeDom.

We as humans will always suffer
injustices. How we deal with
them will determine the outcome
of our lives. In the short term if
we do not learn to Handle them,
it will cost us. In the Long
term we can Learn, and grow
stronger. We can even help other
people if they will but listen.

A baby christan does not do a
good Job at listening. Because
they may have read the Bible
and feel as if they Know all
there is to Know about life
and God.

When other people give them
Words of wisDom. They often
Quote Scripture as words of
knowledge. They believe they are
always right. But Words of
WisDom will always triumph over
Words of knowledge.

No matter how successful we
become in life. If our success
is not founded on wisDom.
Our success will always be
Short lived.

You can hear the AuDible voice of God.
But if you dont respond out of love.
But instead respond out of fear
you will become disobedienT aT
at some point. And run the risk of

Destroying all that you stand for.

Good intentions capture the
mind of Christ. But good Actions
Capture the Heart of Christ.

When your intentions and actions
flow together in a balanced and wise
manner you become mature.
Just know your Knowledge will be
tested by time. and experience
will turn into wisDom. You will
grow strong and be full of
grace. And the Lord will bless
the work of your hand

You may have asked
yourself, like King david.
Why do the wicked seem to
Prosper in the Land? While
the righteous endure hardships.

The Reason is Plain. God is
Grooming the righteous. By
Allowing them to see the foolish
ness of the wicked. God Allows
his people to see the wild spending
and Squandering of riches and
partying lifestyle of the wicked.
So that the righteous can
Learn not to fall victim to
Poverty after the Lord gives
them earthly riches.

He Allows us to see the fruits
of foolishness. . So that we can
avoid the traps. When He sees
it fit to give us a financial increase
and puts us into a position of
Influence. We will be more
responsible. And we shall be
good stewards with what he gives
us.

Just remember this saying a fool
and his riches shall soon part.

It is utter foolishness to be rich
and spend Large sums of money on
Designer clothing and Jewelry and
shoes. The only thing you will
reap from all of those things is
Hote and Jealousy. Driving a Luxury
car through a poor neighborhood is
Just not wise.

Having many friends can
be Just as foolish. Especially
if their Hearts are not right.

God told us to come out
from among them and be ye
separate. that was a warning
from god. How you respond
to that warning will Determine
the outcome of the storm in
your life.

Chapter two

W͟HAT͟ D͟REAMS͟ A͟ C͟HRISTAIN͟ S͟HOULD͟ H͟AVE͟ A͟ND͟ H͟OW TO MAKE͟ T͟HEM COME TRUE͟

In my childhood i was being cared for by
by mennonites. They live their
Lives Similar to the amish. They
do not Watch television. They
normally live in the country and
Grow their own food. They also do
not wear Jewelry or expensive cloThes.

Neither do they participate in
What they would call worldly affairs
Such as military, police work or
government Jobs. or anything that
Would require a college degree.
They also HomeSchool their children.

Many people would call these
people religious extremists. I call
them men and women of faith.

The worldly Justice sysTem
and governmental branches.
Have become corrupt over the LasT
Couple decades. That does not
Mean that we Should not
Participate in it. It only means
that good christains Should
Stand up and fill the Void.

Mennonites believe that tv
is of the devil. Not based on
their own experienced but based
off of what their parents have
told them. I personally disagree,
I believe that tv is watching
more than a Device
It is how you use it
that makes it good or evil.
IF more christan filmmakers
Would rise up and start to flood
the networks we would experience
more sanctified entertainment.

It is because christans Have
Stood by Idly. That is why we
Witness the filth that we
View every day on television.

It is the parents Job to
Set boundaries. When it comes
to what their children watch
on television. There are good
Television networks such as
TBN Hillsong the church channel
and Juice TV. And i believe that
in the future these kind of
networks will become more
common.

It is fear that keeps christains
from expanding their iDeologies
throughout the world we live in.
If christains would become more
bold we could take back this
nation. And reach the four corners
of the world.

We could become what
Christ has commissioned us
to be. Which is the light
of the world.

If you are someone who
is Strong in your christain
faith. And You have a dream
Of becoming a pillar noT JusT
in your own community, but
the World. I am calling you out, to make your Dreams
Come true. Go Write that
Script for the next big christan
movie. Write that book if you
are a teacher, And teach the
nations about the Lord.
Use the gifts and talents
You have to reach this hurting
Lost and Dying World.

If you are a peacemaker
take the necessary legal
classes and pass the bar. So
that you can become a JuDge
or a Lawyer. And make the
World amore Just and safer
place to live in.

To many times i thoughT the
Lord's return was imminent.
Maybe even hours Away from
What i watched on CNN and
fox news. They portray the
Most negative Side of
life. A religious man would believe
The end is near. An extremist
Would believe the time is now.

If you had dreams of being
married and having children.
You Should not abandon these
dreams ouT of fear. Yes the
World has become a dangerous
place, and the wicked seem to
flourish. But if you
don't have children of your own
and raise them up in a christan
home. Where will the next
generation of evangelist and
preacher's come from. It is
your God given duty to be
fruitful and multiply.

Success is not considered
Success in the eyes of the
Unsuccessful. Their eyes are on
the riches instead of the wisdom
it takes to get the riches.
Creating Various problems.

What Dreams a Christain Should Have And How to make them come true

There are many christans
Who believe having money
is Sinful. As a wise born again
Christan. Let me tell you
there is nothing foolish abouT
having money. It is what
you do with that money that can
make you foolish.
IF a christan man takes all
his money and gives it to the
poor, that can be foolish. But if
a Christan man invest his
money in a small business and
gives the poor a Job. That is
wise and it gives the poor
a chance to be a blessing to
others.

If a Christan man invest
his money into a drug and alcohol
Rehab that is wise. And it
is a gift that keeps giving
changing lives.

We must be good stewards
with the Lord's money.
People accuse creflo Dollar of
Hoarding money. But that man
has invested millions of Dollars
back into his community and
communities throughout the
World.

It is mostly baby christans
and Unbelievers who are critical
of mature christans that have
money. Because they
do not understand the dynamics
involved with keeping and
Spending money. In a way that
You can create real change in the
World

Those who prey on the
Wealthy will one day become
the prey of the wealthy.
Those who
Constantly plot on how to
get money without working
for it. Will be deprived of the
Little money and freedom
they have.

When they lose their money
Health and freedom. It will be
the rich who will line their
pockets with their money and
time. So in time if they Do
not change their way of
thinking. They will fall into
the same hands, they robbed
and Whispered evil
about.

The world is Looking to
reward the man or woman.
That can bring true transformation
to the world. Let's look at one
of the greatest leaders of our
times. Billy Graham because of this
one man millions of men and
Women have been touched by
the Gospel. He has impacted
this nation and nations
across the world.

A new day is dawning a transition
is coming. the Lords Awakened
Kingdom servants have Arrived to
take their place, and cReate lasting
Change for the world. Welcome
to the Last generation. The generation that will see the
Coming of the messiah.

Chapter Three

The Reality Of Wars And Rumors Of Wars.

The entire world is reaching
the stage of critical mass.
from the east to the middle east
North, South and West.
All nations are preparing for war.
While leaders of nations and
government officials are chanting
peace and prosperity.

As North Korea makes advantees
in its ballistic missile programs.
It has also tested a hydrogen
bomb. Many times more powerful,
than any of its former nuclear tests.
They have publicly stated that,
they have a missile capable of
Striking anywhere in the Known
World.

Major prophet Kevin Marasi
from Kenya, received a vision
from the Lord concerning this.
In his vision He was taken to
the state of California. Where he
was shown intercontinental ballistic
missiles falling on the state of
California.

Another prophet named Elvi Zapata
received a similar vision from the Lord.
In his vision, he saw Intercontinental
ballistic missiles strike WashinTon.DC.
He said he was told this event world
happened after the rapture.

In the middle east Iranian backed rebels fired
a ballistic missile into Saudi Arabia. fortunately
It was shot down. Weeks later un Ambassador
nikki Haley spoke at the UN. She said this
missile has Irans name written all over it.
She also said a coalition will be formed to
Deal with this issue.

The Reality Of Wars And Rumors Of Wars.

Prophet dumitru duduman received
A Vision from the Lord. In his vision
He saw China, Russia Iran, and Korea have
an allegiance. To come together
to destroy america and rule the world
themselves.

China is North Korea's Ally. If America
Were to attack North Korea. China Would
not sSit by iDly. Also Russia and Iran
are also ally's. This prophecy give to
dumitru is very realistic.

So how close are we to the
Accurate fulfillment of these prophecies.

According to many moDern day
prophets. Such as Sa dHu Sundar
We are not that far away at all.
According to Sadhu Sundar. We were
given a four year reprieve. Starting
at the beginning of 2016. Ending in
2021. This four year window is
a chance for America and the rest of the
World to repent. Judgement would
Ultimately come in the year 2022.
Well Known prophet terry bennett
Said there would be a one world
Religion established around thAt time.

Pope francis has taken unprecedented
Actions to unify the religions around the
World. He said that all paths lead to
heaven. He Also Said that by being a
good person you can enter into the
Kingdom of Heaven. He has deliberately
Shunned the Scripture that said no man
Comes to the father except through the
Son.

The Lord has revealed
the truth to many prophets concerning
Pope francis.

Here is a Prophetic revelation
given to SadHu SunDat October 2016.
The pope will Join hands with a
political World leader to establish a
One World Religion of peace. This new
Religion will remove all the barriers
of race, caste, and creed. As A Result
it will be Accepted by All the worlds
political leaders as it will promote
guaranteed peace.

Famous televangelist Jack Van impri
has Also Spoken OUT against this
false religion the pope is promoting.
Jack said it would be called
Chrislam a combination of christanity
and Islam.

Prophet terry bennett saw a
persecution coming to the cathlic
church.He saw many christans put
to death for their rebellion against
this false Religion.

So what does this mean? It
means we are on the edge of eternity.
When they say peace and safety
SuDDen Destruction will come on them.

This generation is facing unprecedented
Challenges. Let me be clear this is
the generation that shall by no means
pass before Seeing the coming of the
Messiah.

In December 2017 Donald trump
made a public Announcement.
Declaring Jerusalem as the eternal
capital of Israel. This statement
received Heavy criticism and
backlash. The pope spoke against
Donald trump decision. Also the
leader of palestine. He said because
This Act there will be no peace and
that what will come from this ACT.
The leader of palestine called for
three Days of Violence against
Israel.

As we see the threat of war
and false religion spread throughout
our world. We as christians must
stand up and take back the world.
Hearts will fail men from the fear that
is gripping them. We must be
Courageous and Stand for what we
believe in and never Compromise the
truth.

Chapter Four

YOUTUBE PROPHETS

If you were to go online and
Vist youtube and type in the
Word rApture. You would see Hundreds
if not thousands of prophecies
about the Rapture or end of Time events.

A lot of the prophets that are
Predicting end time events. Are operating
Out of the second Heaven. The Second
heaven is where the schemes of the
Evil one is being Planned. Principalities
and rulers of darkness congregate in
this area. To Plan the destruction
Of mankind.

Many Well meaning Prophets are
hearing voices from that area abouT
the future of mankind. A lot of
their prophecies fail. Because the
enemy's plans are not Gods
Plans.

Some of these prophecies come
true but not at the time the
The Prophet Says.

For example there was a prophet
that said there would be an economic
collapse in the fall of 2017.
This event did not occur.

It is not to say there will
not be an economic collapse.
Because there will be, Just
not at the time the prophet
preDicted it to be.

Some times god changes the
Dates of an expected calamity
because a nation repents ot he
gives them a chance to
repent.

I am not delegitimizing youtube
Prophets. Because there are a lot
of true prophecies that have come
to pass from this platform. There
are also many prophets that have clearly
been deceived.

I remember listening to one
of these prophets say he was
one of the two witnesses and
that god taught him karate and
He would soon take his place
at the temple mount breathing fire
Upon his enemies. I had to laugh
When I heard this, but he made it
Sound so convincing that i thought
it might actually be true. He even
back it up with Scripture.

Now Let's get back to true prophecies
and prophets

There is A female prophet
Who has received Visions and
Dreams from the Lord. She has
had many revelations imparted
to her through the Holy Spirit.
Concerning end times.

In one of Her reveLations
She was Shown the greaT tribulation
She was told that the price
Of food Would far exceed the price
We Would normally pay for food.
It was A hundred Dollars for JusT
one piece of meat.

The women also spoke of technology
that would exist in the future.
She said Some people would be injected
With nano bots that could Alter
the DnA of the person infected.
She went on to speak of a transportation
System that could reach anywhere

in the Know world in less than
an hour. She also sAw holograms
That was as common as television.
She also Spoke of seeing a new energy
Source.

This Lady was also Shown
ADvanced weapons systems. And
She saw the mark of the beast being
implemented. She saw a military
force pushing people into lines
to purchase food clothing and
Cosmetics. The soldiers were extremely
Hostile toward the people and some
of them were, executing people on
site.

She was shown chinse and
RussiAn troops occupying the
U.S. mainland. And according to what
she saw they were mercilessly
killing American citizens.

Another famous Youtube Prophet
I spoke of elvi zapata earlier as.
He was take into Heaven
Were the Lord Showed him
Elvis Presley Whintey Houston
and Tupac Shakur.

When he beheld Elvis
He was upseT. He said lord,
This man was a drug addict
and a racisT. How is it that
is he in the KingDom? The Lord
Looked at him Sternly and said
Who are you to JuDge my
Servant. The Lord went on to
say. Elivs Presley had a good
heart and that he lives a
rough life.

He was then showed
Witney houston. He saw that
She had on a garment of
praise. He saw that she had
music wrapped around Her.
The robe was singing praises
to the Lord. She now occupies
a place in heaven as a worship leader.

Not only was he shown these
two extraordinary people. He was
also shown tupac Shakur!!
He said the Lord showed Him.
The events that took place
Around the time tupac was shot.
He was shown tupac bleeding Out
on the sidewalk. He Heard tupac
Say to the Lord, Dont let me
Die in these Streets Alone. Jesus
then appear and Held Him in His Arms
and prepared to tAke him into the
Kingdom.

Before The Apocalypse

Chapter Five

PROPHET OR MENTAL PATIENT

Throughout the Bible
Prophets of old were thought to
be mad men. Which is Just
Another name for LunaTic.

I personally do.Not believe there
are too many modern day prophets.
That have not experienced some
form of Psychosis, or at leasT
have been labled Such by Society.
It Just comes with the
territory. Also it gives me an
understanding Why The bible says
a prophet is not Accepted in
his hometown.

As i have Covered in the Previous
Chapters. A lot of Prophets and Prophetess
are operating in the Second Heaven.
There is a lot of Confusion and Darkness
that operated in that realm. Which
is the cause of much mental confusion

On earth today. The third Heaven
is where we as prophets need
to be operating. But in orDer to go
to the third Heaven we musT
first pass through the second
Heaven.

Sometimes well meaning christans
Hear what they would call a word
of Knowledge about future events
and think it is coming from the
lord. Sometimes we are deceived.

The Lord does speak at times.
Sometimes audible and Sometimes
a Impression on our hearts. BuT it
we hear a-word from the Lord.
Concerning bad events that will take
Place. But we don't hear a Word
concerning the outcome and how
it will give God the glory.
Chances are we have been
deceived.

When i first received the
gift of prophecy. I was a very
troubled individual. I often had
night Mares and the enemy was
Working overtime to keep me
trapped in the Second Heaven, Were
Confusion Dwells. So that i
Would not receive the full
revelation the Lord was
trying to send me.

I was hospitalized on
numerous occasions and put
on Psychiatric medication.
I Knew that what i was hearing
was coming from a Source
outside of myself. But doctors
Kept saying that i basically have
an overactive imagination, and
a chemical imbalance. They said
my mind made these voices. But
I knew my mind could not mimick
he intelligent conversations
that I had with these entities.

For example when the Lord would
spoke to me i knew it was him.
I would hear the Love and
Compassion in his voice. Which i knew
my mind could not Just mimic.
If these were Just my thoughTs
like the Doctors were saying how
I never thought about them before.

1The gift of discernment is
Something thaT must be developed
over time. It is not Something
that Just Appears or is given to
you. From trial and error you
learn to recognize the voice of the
enemy.

Now i am not saying that
Mental health doctors are
fraudes. But i am saying that
the source of which the
Psychologist claims the voices
are coming from simply is not
the source.

Even the psychologist will
tell you. There is no cure for
these illnesses. Only a practice
and these practices only
temporarily treat the problem.

Sometimes when a patient
is treated. They are so overly
medicated, that they can barely
Function in society. I'm not
saying that someone who
suffers from mental illness should
not be treated. But i Am saying
The medication Should not be Abused.

A Stumbling block for young Prophets
and prophetess is marijuana. for
Someone who is trying to Dicern
the voice of the Lord from
the voice of the enemy this
can be disastrous.

I speak from experience.
Years ago when i was in my
early to mid twenties. I was smoking
marijuana. I was operating a lot in
the second Heaven where the
rulers of Darkness and principalities
dwell. The Lord would sometimes
Send a messenger to me to tell
me to stay away from this
Substance. So that i could
clearly hear the Lord. But i
Would not listen. I was told time and
Time again that marijuana was not always a good thing.

One day i picked up a
book written by Mary K baxter
Called the Divine revelation of
the Spirit realm. In This book
it talked about a young women
Who Smoked marijuana. It said
at first she only Smoked on
occaitions with her friends. Then
it showed how in the spirit realm
a demon was orchestrating the
Whole thing. The demon in the
Spirit realm placed a rope around
the girls neck when she first
Started using it. Then the rope
was turned into a chain causing
an addiction.

The once beautiful
young girl. turned into a pot
head and her beauty was tarnished.

You may be saying to yourself.
This is a harmless substance.
Maybe you are saying This is
not a drug. I can assure you
that if you do not forsake it.
You will find yourself on a path
to Destruction.

The demonic forces in the 2nd
Heaven love nothing more than to
Keep our future prophets and
Prophetess bound by different
Substances. To keep Them from
Operating in the third Heaven.
And to keep them from becoming
the men and women god called
them to be.

IF there is anything else
I could tell you to help you.
Its to stop now before you
ruin your life. Life itself as of
today requires you put the pot
down.

Another Pittfall for young
prophets and prophetess is
AlcohoL. Prophets are very Sensitive
to the Spirit World. Making their
minds very vulnerable to the
deception of evil SpirTS.

When a Seer is under the
influence of these Substances
the evil spirits have
more control over their mind.

Alcohol is A downer. When
a prophet who operates in the
Spirit realm uses Alcohol He or
She often times battles the Spirit of
depression and then Suicide
It does not always start ouT
that way. Normally the evil spirit
lets you have a little fun before
Putting the noose around your neck.
You will come to find out that after

a few days of drinking. It just isnt
as fun as it used to be. Then later
Drinking will Just be down right
boring. Then it will start to
be depressing. Later you will start
having Suicidal thoughts. That
you might act on if you donoT
get help.

This is why the bible says
There is pleasure in sin for a Season,
but its end result is death.
JeSuS was trying to warn us
of the deception the enemy uses
against us.

I hope you will be wise and
free yourself from these Swares
and Overcome. By the blood of the
Lamb and the word of your
testimony. If you Do, the Lord
will exalt you into a higher Spiritual
level.

Chapter Six

PROPHECIES AND SUICIDE

The Job of a prophet is
very serious. Lives hang in
the balance. As a prophet
we must be sure we are
getting our visions and dreams
and words of knowledge.
From the third heaven where
Jehovah and Christ dwell.

Because many prophets are
getting their knowledge from
the second Heaven. Where
darkness resides. They are getting
what i would like to call dark
prophecies.

Some of these prophecies
are So negative and without
hope_that, the people and
The Prophet receiving Them
feels a great deal of Hopelessness.

In extreme cases propheTS
and receiver of prophecies
feel so hopless that they
take their own lives. I speaK
of this as Someone Who has
attempted Suicide many times.

Thank god I was never Successful.
I realize the enemies attempT
to overwhelm my mind with
dark prophecies, To the piont that
i believed life was not Worth
living.

Let me tell those of you who
may be suffering from Suicidal thoughts.
You are fearfully and wonderfully
made. No one on earth is like
you. You are Gods masterpiece.
Even though you have your short
comings. The Lord has died for
you and all of your transgressions

Past, Present and future.

ou do not have to fear god
though fearing god is the
beginning of wisDom it is not
the end. For perfect love cast
out, all fear.

The Only reason that fear is
the beginning of wisDom. Is
because you do not yet Know
Jesus. Once you get to Know
the Lord the fear will leave
and peace will consume you.

You must Know that he is a deity
of pure and unconditional love.
It will be his love that will
transform you into his likeness
not his fear.

If you are a prophet and you
are not living in his love.
But you are trying To live up to
What you believe his standards
are. You will always fall shorT.
You must resT in the finished
Works of Christ. Until he takes
the desires that are contrary to
his spirit from you.

A Pastor who i owe a lot to
for what he has taught me is
Joseph prince. Joseph prince booK
entitled destine to reign. Has
given me the right Prospective
on life in christ, and how to be
an overcomer. This book has
dramatically changed my life.
I Know it will do the same for
you.

Prophecies and Suicide

A lot of times when Christans
Come to Christ. They are mentally
out of shape. They have experienced
a hard ungodly life, and they
are looking for change. Some of
them have used or are still
using drugs and Alcohol to cope.
And some MAY be suffering
from mental illness.

I needed to be on psych
meds because of my mental illness.
Do I believe that Jesus heals?
The answer is yes!! I believe
that Jesus heals people personally,
and sometimes through
the medication that doctors give.
For anyone to say otherwise.
It is very dangerous. We can
not Just expect Jesus to Heal
us personally, When Sometimes
He operates through medication.

We cannot be prideful or
arrogant When it comes to
the way that Jesus wants to
heal us. We must Accept whaT
is offered to us and be grateful.

Do not despise Small beginnings
because in the end you will
receive whatever you ask for.

I did not want to be on physic
meds. Because some of them cause
you to gain a little or a lot of weighT.
And also people tend to criticis
you for taking medicine for
psychiatric purposes.

I have heard it all when it
Comes to the critics voicing
their opinions. Some of them said
I dont need medicine. If my mind
was strong enough, or if i was such
a good christan i would not
medication.

I took their advice and
I stopped taking medication.
I trust Jesus for a personal
Healing. I even had four of five
Preachers Lay hands on me.

To make a Long story short
I ended up in and Out of
mental hospitals. I had a
Psychotic episode and ended
up burning down my own
Apartment building that
was fully Occupied. Smoke
Damage Destroyed the
neighboring buildings. Causing
Over 2 million Dollars Worth
of damage. I was arrested
and charged with aggravated
arson. And I am now writing
this book from inside Albion
State correctional Institution in
Albion PA.

If i would have Just listened
to the lord and the DocTors
about needing to take my
medication i would not be
here today.

Do i think god can turn this
around for my good? Yes buT
needless to say i would not have
to go through all of these
Unnecessary changes. If i would
have listened to the Doctors
God Appointed to help me in my
Time of need.

Another facade is that vitamins
can treat Scizoeffective
disorder. Vitamins i repeat vitamins
can by no means treat that DisorDer.
they may help you from getting it
but once you have it you better
get the right medication.

I have heard a lot of people
Say that is a man or a women
Commits Suicide they will go
to hell. That is not
always the case. Mentally ill
People do not Know right from
Wrong their mind is trapped
in the Darkness of the Second
Heaven. Charles Stanley had a
revelation that people who
are in this Condition.
Do make it into heaven they jusT
Do not receive any rewards.
Probley from their lack of
Obedience.

So if you have last a love
one to suicide. Through Untreated
mental illness you can rest assure
if they were a believer they are
in heaven with Christ.

Sometimes we have lost
friends and family members
from Suicide. We may not have
even considered that they were
suffering From a mental illness.
Were they Drinking heavily? Were
they unreasonably Angry or
Anti Social. Were they suffering
from insomnia. Were they
extremely sad or depressed.
These are signs of a mental illness.

I had a cousin named Darrell
Who commited suicide. Two
Weeks before he died. He came to
me and said Busta that is my
nickname. I just can't stop thinking
every Day i go to my room and my
mind races I just start to Drink
looking for relief, and i just get
more depressed.
He basically told me he was
having suicidal thoughts.

I was in mental Anguish
myself. I told Him in tired
of living and He basically told
me life has become unbearable
to him as well. Two weeks
later, I was told that He
Accidentally shot himself.
But i knew the truth.

It Hurt me inside but in
a way I envied him. You see my friends
mental trauma, Is a physical
pain in the mind. not Just
mental Anguish. I was so
conflicted Inside that i could
not even go to his funeral. To
this day I feel like i was the
cause of his Death. If i could have
Just been a little more Stronger
maybe i could Have helped him.

Months later i had an open
Vision. I seen my cousin
Darrell. I Asked him did He
make it to heaven he smiled
and said yes I did.

Later on in my life i would
Hear his auDible voice.
Saying to me everything is
going to be alright. He would
always speak to me during
Various trails in my life. now
I know I will see him again.

Let me be clear for those of
you who are suffering from mental
illness i know the pain you feel.
Suicide is not a way out. You will
hurt your family and friends If
you choose that route. You have
been called to a higher calling. not
many people can say they hear the
audible voice of the lord or
that they receive visions.

Prophecies and Suicide

The Lord Wants to see you
prosper and grow. He wants
to see you raise a family and
be successful in life. And
teach your children the ways
of God. The enemy will do all
he can to Sabotage your future.
Do not allow that to happen.
TAke your medication, and
if you feel like you are overly
medicated. Tell your doctor,
and he will change your dosage
to where you can function properly.

Allow God to heal you the way
he chooses. Do not be religious
and prideful to the way that
the Lord chooses to operate.
Your future and the future of
those around you depends on
it.

Chapter Seven

F̲U̲T̲U̲R̲E̲ C̲H̲R̲I̲S̲T̲A̲N̲S̲

It is fear that keeps Christans
from becoming all that they are
called to be. If you feel the world
is too evil to have children in.
You will not become a parent.
If you fear that Jesus is coming
at any moment you. You will not
prepare yourself to become successful
in your life here on this earth.

These are the mistakes of
the lasT generation. But it does not
and will not be the mistakes of
this generation.

There is a generation that
will do mighty exploits for the
lord. They will exhibit
Spiritual Strength and Courage
not Seen on earth. Since the
days of pentecost

Pentecost is the time when
the disciples set out to spread
the gospel to the four corners of
the world. This was accompanied
With miracles signs and Wonders. .
Also with Courageous hearts that
feared nothing. And Saw death as
gain.

The consequences of these
brave men and women preaching
during those times of fierce
opposition. Is the reason the
 gospel is Known. And is touching
the Lives of millions across the
World. It is the reason why
This Season is harvest time.

As Jesus said the harvest
is great. But the Workers are few
Pray then that more are sent.

We have seen blood moons.
Also we have seen Solar eclipses
and earthquakes and storms at
Unprecedented levels. So what
comes nexts.

The next move of god will be
revival. This is a great move of god
Accompanied with Wars and natural
disasters. That will bring us into
the great tribulation. Followed by
the millennial reign. Which is
When god comes to earth and
establishes his Kingdom for a thousand
years.

There is an army of the Lord
that is rising up. That will do greater things than what the
Lord has done. Just as he said
they would.

Some of these Christans will
have the ability to fly and teleport
and use telepathy to communicate. .
They will speak and the Atmosphere
will change. Angelic power will
be distributed to each one of them.

In a Vision i saw Jonathan
Cahn Jewish author of the Harbinger
and the paradigm.HE was left behind as
one of the 144,000. Preaching in a
large Stadium to those who were
left behind.

What we are starting to see.
Is the beginning of Sorrows.
But do not fear God has a great
plan for us in all of this.

As the earth plunges deeper
into the dark. The light
will shine that much brighter.
Gods children and any one who
wants to be taught by God. Will
experience the full weight of
Gods glory.

We as christans must take hold
of gods hand and let him lead
us through these dark and trying
times. As we do we will grow.
Proverbs 18:10 The name of the
Lord is a Strong tower the
righteous run into it, and Are Safe.

The father has spoken to
his people. As they listen and
respond. The people will rise into
new levels of understanding. When
the understanding levels have reached
high enough. It will bring
transformation and purification to

The body of Christ. And entire
nations will be transformed.
before Our Very eyes.

I personally, based on the
Prophetic revelations given to
me. I have seen America rise
to a level of prosperity such as
this world has never seen.
Followed by a poverty common
to places Such as ethiopiA.

We are at the begging of a
golden Age. Here in america
I will share a vision i witnessed
Concerning the prosperity of
America . In this Vision i was
taken a few years into the future.
I saw fresh paved streets and
a buildings, that seemed to
shimmering and Glowing. It seemed
to be Alive. I was a bright light.

The people I saw were very happy.
They were full of Joy and expectation
it looked as if they were shining
with the light of god. All of a suDDen time froze they started
Staring into the sky as if something
Grand was about to happen. End
of vision.

To all of you christans prophesying
dark days ahead for america. I must
tell you light comes first. Then darkness
falls. You are not going to get away
that easy. You must first answer
the call on your life. First you should
set out to accomplish the dreams
God put in your heart as a child.
Such as marriage, college and worK.
Then you should use your work
to give god the glory. After you
have accomplished these things you
will have the Joy of Knowing you
were chosen for a time such as this.

And you raise your children
up to Know the same. So
that they can be like you a
blessing to a Whole generation.
And a testimony to an entire
nation.

It is up to us as Christans
to give god the glory, and be
who he has called us to be.
Praying in tongues will be vital
to the next move of god.
Kingdom Soldiers will operate
in mighty signs and Wonders
after praying for hours in the
Spirit.

There is coming a time when
believers will not be allowed
to meet Publicly.
The believers will be lead by the
holy Spirit and he will tell them
What to say and where to go.

Many Prophets have been Speaking
Up, And telling the World. That
the Lord is birthing Something new
through his People. It is an
Urgent call to a new Position
of authority in the earth.

Deuteronomy 30:19
Today I have given you the
Choice between life and death,
between blessing and cures. now,
call heaven and earth to witness
the Choice that you make. oh
that you would choose live so that
your descendants would live.

If there is a problem that you
have been praying to the Lord to
take Care of. now is the time
for break through.

Maybe you are tired of the
typical christan experience.
Maybe you are hungry for the
Supernatural. The lord is calling
out to you right now. If you
Would Just pray in the Spirit.
You would see an overflow of
the Supernatural like never
before. Do not just think, your
Pray will be answered without
you playing your role.

The Glory of the Lord is
About to affect every part of
the Secular World. From movies
music, Industry and businesses.
there is coming men and Women
of god that will rise up in these
areas. They will dominate under
the power of the Lord. Creating
a Lasting Change here in
America.

Chapter 8 Eight

ETERNITY IN THE BALANCE

Eternity is in the balance for many souls. Who will only be saved during the great tribulation. For many, coming to Christ will cost them their lives.

We are blessed to be Able to Come to christ with almost little to no persecution here in america. In other countries Christans are not so fortunate. Other Christans wAnt to come to christ but they are not willing to give up their sins.

The church here in america is full of sin. It will take revivAl and Judgment to shake this nation. And Awake them from their Spiritual Slumber. What is even more Shocking is that even when the worst of Judgements strike People

Will Still refuse to repent. They
will shake their fast and curse
God.

We are reaching a climax in the
World as far as sin is concerned.
It is time for christan to
wake up and realize eternity is
in the balance. As a nation we
stand Parallel to the roman
empire right before its fall.
Our military like the roman military
is spread across the world in
Various conflicts. And like the roman society
immorality is ramped in our nation.
  The only thing that is Keeping
this nation from severe judgment
is Our Commitment to what is real
and a remnant of christans
Praying for revival.

If revival does not breakout
soon, War will. Just as in the
days of ancient is real when immorality
reached its height. So it is with
america. We have two super
powers that smile in our face. But
Secretly do everything in their
power to Undermine us socially
and economically. the two allies
of these nation openly express
their hatred for us, and their
Intentions to destroy this country.
This is reality.

I do believe there will be a
Wealth transfer. Just as Kenneth
Copeland said there would be.
I personally believe that it will
happen differently. I believe the
Wealth transfer will happen when
the rapture takes place. I also believe
the wealth transfer is happening
now.

When trump took office, the
Wealth of ungodly nations was
Starting to come back to this nation.
Unfortunately this nation has
become ungodly. When the rapture.
takes place a lot of the food and
material possessions. Will go to
the new believers. That is the
Wealth transfer i see coming.

A well Known televangelist
who goes by the name Perrystone
has gone on television and
said that the hebrew year
5778 Which is 2018 in america
signifies the beginning of Jacobs
troubles.

I do not know if this is true
 or not but i Know the lord
has had enough with the
Wickedness of this world.

I Also Know that great natural
disasters famines and Wars are
Coming to this Planet.In the misT
of all these things we will wittness
the greatest revival the world
has ever seen.

If there was ever a season
to look up and know that your
Salvation draweth near, it is here.
Glorious things are on the horizon.
And eternity is hanging in the
balance. Will you hear the trumpet
blast or will you be left behind it
is all up to you

Just as there are children
of the light. There are also
Children of Darkness.
You may ask yourself when will
God punish the wicked. Just
remember you were Wicked at
one time too. The Lord is
giveing the same chance
He gave you.

If you call yourself a christan
you should be grateful, to see
God redeem your brother from
his sins. Remember one thing
Dear Children of god if someone
does wrong. They can be redeemed.

A lot of the most evil people
are called to the highest positions
in the body of christ. They must
only come to christ and
mature.

Do not ever give up hope
on your family and friends.
That does not mean you should
Keep company with them. Sometimes
it is best to love them at a
distance. And continually pray
for them. It is the best thing
we can do for them. And when
they come to christ they will be
your best companions.

A time is coming when the mosT
evil people will give their lives
to Christ. Just like the
Apostle Paul they will see the
error in their ways. They will go on
to transform nations and bring HunDreds
of thousands if not millions to the Lord.

We must look beyond the
temporal things and gaze inTo
the future. Nobody Would have
ever dreamed that Apostle Paul
PersEcutor of christains, would
become a Christan himself.

Eternity hangs in the balance
lives are on the line. We
must plant seeds. Wherever there
is soil and pray for the Crops to
grow.

One day if you are patient and
diligent. You will experience a
harvest hundred fold. Just keep on
believing and praying and one
day. God will reward you for
your trails. In this life and in
The next.

Eternity in the Balance

Eternity makes time look
petty. We all must stand the test
of time. If we have our minds
set on eternity. And we chase
our dreams. Time will be nothing
but a drop in the bucket. MY Advice
to you is to chase your dreams.
A dreamless life can lead to
Poverty And destruction.

Chapter Nine

IN MEMORY OF THE FALLEN

I dedicate this chapter to
our men and women of faith
who fell from great Heights.
But they refused to stay down
and let the devil win.

They went on to do great
works for the body of Christ.
They overcame the devil through
the blood of the lamb and the
Word of their testiMOny.

Jim baker was accused of stealing
money and adultery either in the
late 80s or early 90s he was
sentenced to 5 years in prison.
Where it was Just him and the
Lord. Mr Baker was A televangelist
and his name was great at that
time. When people like Mr baker
fall from grace. There are always
scoffers and mocker that come

Out of the Wood work and
Point their fingers and say
i told you so Just look at him
now.

Jim Baker is human like you
and me the only difference is
 his life is on public display.
He is not fool proof. Just like
he fell so can you. And if
we do not have a relationship
with Jesus you will at Some point
fall to. You can be a preacher or A
teacher. But if your relationship
With Jesus is not a personal one
you will fall too.

When Mr baker was incarcerated
he learned to have a personal relationship
With the lord. He wrote a book around the time of his
incarceration entitled. I was wrong.

Jim baker has gone through
some rough times. But he
has come out victorious.

Jim currently host his own
tv show called the Jim baker
Show. He is the leader and a
pillar in his own community.
He is doing a good Job of informing
People about end time events.
He now has a purpose given to him
by the lord himself. To feed
the christans that will be
left behind during the great
tribulation.

Not only that he sends food
to hurting people around the World.
Who are suffering from natural
disasters and Government oppression

This is a man that has come
out of the fire of trials and
tribulation. He is shining in
the image of our Creator.
May God continue to bless that
man, and the works of his hand.

Jimmy Swagger is another legendary
televangelist that fell from grace.
He Apparently did some lewd
act with some women other than
his wife.

Jimmy Swagger got on national
tv while crying and weeping. He said
He had sinned against god. This
is a man that fervently preached
against the same act that he was
accused of. He mercilessly attacked
and spoke against sin and sinners.
One of the reasons that i believe
these men sinned againsT God isnt so
much the lewd acts they
committed. But the real sin in
Their lives were legalism. Having
a holier than thou attitude.

Both Jim and Jimmy Would
get on television and Viciously
attack sinners. Instead of trying
to build them up. They preached
fire and brimstone message.

I am no stranger to the fire
and brimstone Preaching.

When i lived with the mennonites
as a child. A fire and brimstone
message was the only message i
heard. we lived without television
the women wore dresses similar to
the pilgrims. and they covered
their heads with bonnets or veils.

We lived in our own communities
with little, to no outside
influence.

It is easy to live in a community
with little to no outside influence.
And preach a fire and brimstone
message. But if you live in the real
World you are going to need
grace to see you through.

Preachers and teachers who live out
here in the real world will sometimes
Stumble. the more fame and money
you got. the easier it will be to
fall. We are told to be in the
World and not of it. So i give
the mennonites credit for that.

Unfortunately a lot of mennonites have
fallen into legalism and self righteousness.
They have a Unrealistic view of
the world around them. They are very
timid people

In Memory Of The Fallen

It takes courage to live in
the, Wordly World as they would
call it. It is not for the faint
hearted. Though a righteous man
may fall seven times they get
back up again. But when the
Wicked fall they are utterly
Destroyed.

I have yet to see a wicked man
in the menninte community.
But i have seen wicked men in ours.

There are some who Know the
truth but still hold on to their
evil ways. They have gone their
whole lives without repenting

One of those people who
has blind the massed was
pope Benidict. According to one
near death testimony from
Angelica. She saw the Pope
in hell. According to her testimony
and the testimony of a few others.

Pope Benidict was an evil man.
He stole the glory that should
only be given to God. He also
like many catholics was an idol
worshiper.

But let me be clear you must
endure to the end if you want to
become victorious in this christan
life.

If you are a chirstan living
In this modern world. You either
have or will fall short of the glory
of God. You must put on the full Armor of god and do all you
can to withstand the wiles of
the evil one.

A Lot of people have made
the same mistakes. The People
I have spoken About have made.
The only difference is they live in
the spot light. So their mistakes
are open for all to see.

Chapter Ten

MESMERIZED BY THE WORLD

When I first Left the Mennonites
and came into the Worldly World.
I thought i was in paradise.
Living with the mennonites i was
held back from secular activities.

For example when i was with
the mennonites i was only allowed
one piece of candy after Lunch
and Supper. I also we did not
watch television or Play Video
games

When i went back to the worldly
World. I saw candy that i never
Seen before. Television was
a maGical experience for me. I also
got to play with other african
american children. It was a culture
Shock for me. the only
African american children i played
with before that was my cousin
Shayna.

One of my first experience
with an african American girl
named Ariel. I looked at her and
her tongue was blue from Sucking
on a blow Pop. I was curious
as into whaT made her tongue
blue. So i said to her hey how
Did your tongue get blue?

Immediately her cousin Marilyn
said to me. Are you being funny?
or mocking my cousin. I said
no i JusT Wondered how her
tounge got blue. That
Sparked the first fight i ever
been in. Marilyn immediately
Jumped on me and started
Punching and kicking me.
I had no experience on fighting.
The menninities never fought and
none of their children fought or
even knew how to.

Later on in my life people
would come up to me, and tell
me what my life would have been
life if i would have stayed with
the mennonites. Sometimes i Agree
with them. But the truth is i have
found more powerful christans
out here in this world.

The mennonites do not operate
in the gifts of the Spirit. They
do not believe in praying in tongues
or prophesying. And they are very
critical of each other. If they
do not believe they are living
Up to their Spiritual Standards.

I have seen Miracles take
Place out here in this World.
I have witnessed Prophecies come
to pass out here that the
Mennonites Shun.

I see the reason God called
me out here in this world.
The people remind me of the
People in Ancient israel. Bustling
around buying their worldly Goods.
Trying to make a name for
theirselves. Some of the People
are carrying burdens. Or are sick
from various diseases or are
mesmerized by drugs and
Alchohol.

It is a ruff world but we need
Courageous People who will come out and
Heal the sick, Strengthen the needy
We cannot Just go to the Country
Somewhere and Visit the poor and the
Afflicted on rare occasions. There
is a calling for those who would
get out of their comfort zone and
do what Jesus did. Jesus did not
Just live Somewhere away from
Society. He came into society and

Set it free.

A lot of the mennonites i Know
Would rather Sit in their houses.
And talk about how evil the World
is.And how wicked television is
but they never even experienced
it for themselves.

Yes there is negative things
that happen in the World.But if
the church was living up the the
Standards of the Churches, in the
New testament. We would see more
breakthroughs and Healings and
the awesome Power of the lord.

The Church is the reason why
the world is the way it is. There
are too many passive timid christans.
Who would rather talk about than
be-about. If we see someone doing
wrong we should tell them it is wrong and
encourage them to do right.

We are the keepers of this earth.
It is up to us to make a change
and to make A better future for
tomorrow's generation.

There are many things in this
World that can keep us sidtracked.
But there is nothing that keeps
us sidetracked that we can not use
for our good. .

Whether its technology industry
Or anything else that exist in the
World we are meant to be its
master. Not to let it master us.
If man Would put god first in
his life. There would be nothing
Wrong with recreational sports and
Hobbies. Its when man forgets
God and started to love the things
in the World more than the creaTor,
That is where the problem lies.

There are something in this
World that Should always
be rejected. Such as drugs and
Strong alcohol. I Would put all
Alcohol into the category. But
according to Scriptures Jesus
turned in to Grape Juice like
Jack Van impri said, or was it
alcoholic wine. I guess we
will have to ask the lord. When
we get to heaven. But whether
it was Alcoholic or Alcoholic
We Should use iT in moderation
and all will be well for us.

This world can mesmerize young
men or women. I lost my
virginity at the age of 14. I was
so caught up in hiphop and R and B.
That i cast aside right and wrong
to fulfill what i thought was right
or at least felt right.

A lot of people are caught up
into the hip hop and rock and roll
lifestyle.
The people who are entertaining
this generation, are looking to
Money as the answer of all their
Problems.

They promote sexuall and
violent behavior through their
music. The fatherless teenagers
grab onto it and start living
a lifestyle that they were never
created to live. This leads to
broken homes through drugs and
teenage pregnancies and all sorts
of bitterness and malice. Both
Sides suffer in the end. Both entertainer and the ones being
entertained.

There are Some Christain
hip hop Artist who are
looking to create a change in the
entertainment industry. Such
as Lecre and triplee. Their
music is upbeat and chrisT
centered. I still do not
believe it has a place in the church.
But as far as reaching the
youth, it is a powerful tool. It
gets the masses Attention.

There is a need for more
Christan entertainment in this
World. I would like to see
More mainstream Hiphop Artist
like Drake and Nikki take
this christan entertainment route.
Just imagine what would
Happen if mainstream artist
Like the ones i Just mentioned
Suddenly Shifted to Christan
entertainment. It would start a revival.

Unfortunately a lot of mainstream
artist. Are not willing to
make that change. Because it
would take away from their
glory. And pride is an obsTical
for them.

I do prophesy that in the
not so distant future. We
will see that transformation
come to pass. It will shake
the music inDusty and led
too many Souls being Saved.

Chapter Eleven

Held Captive By Religion.

There are many people today
held captive by religion.
Many well meaning christans
are putting themselves under the
bondage of the law.

There are many other christans
Who turn New testament Gospel
into bondage by not allowing
Grace to have its way With
them. They believe they can
live up to the Standards of the
New testament. When its religious
requirement are even more burden
Some than the old testament.

Many other people are so
religiously brainwashed that they
refuse to live and enjoy
their lives. Some people say things
like you cant wear Jewelry or
fly clothes or watch tv.

There is good things in both of
these things. You JusT cannot
let them consume you.
Neither can you be so consumed
by religion that you miss its
purpose for your life.

The gospel is supposed to
enhance your quality of life, not
Diminish it. The gospel is supose
to set you free, not keep you
bound.

If you find that you are at
War with yourself and the
World. Chances are you have
become Self righteous. And
you have bound yourself bound
by rules. That on your best
day you could not Keep. Instead
of allowing christ to
forgive your short comings, and give
you the grace to walk humbly before him.

Held Captive By Religion.

You have made for yourself an Image
of godliness that only christ
himself could walk out.

A self righteous mindset is
not good after falling to reach
What you believe is personally
the standard for your every
day living. You begin to despair.
Which soon turns into depression
leading to Suicidal thoughTs.
You start on earth falling short of
What you believe, is the standard
set for you.

Before The Apocalypse

Let me be clear if you have
Used the bible to tear yourself
down to nothing, or to uphold your
own holyness without looking
to christ as the beginning and end
of your faith. You need to read
Joseph prince book entitled
destined to reign. It will
transform your life.

During my Incarceration i have
Seen. Many people inbondage to
religion while suffering from mental
illness. One of my best friends
Mr Lamar evans was one of those
people. Every morning and Sometimes
at night he would beat himself
and scream out lord have mercy
on me a sinner.

Held Captive By Religion.

When i moved into his cell,
I could tell that he was not
properly medicated. He had
an unrealistic viewpoint of God.
He thought the Lord was
punishing him for the life
He took in self defense. He
was not at peace with him
Self.

After a couple of months I
Convinced him to get an increase
in his medication. He got his
medication. And Let me tell
you he is a changed man.

He laughs and sometime
Jokes around. He has become
a totally different person.
I see him becoming a Spiritual
leader one day.

Let me tell you mental illness
is serious. If a mental ill person
does not receive treatment.
You will either become a victim
or victimize someone elese.

You can Pray for 3 million hours
it will get you no where you
must get the proper medical
treatment. God does not always
answer our prayers. And if you
feel as if you Deserve Prayers to be
answered. Chances are they wonT
be. Praying for a mental illness to
be healed without treatment
is almost a hopeless cause.

There are rare cases of mental illness
being cured. But that is exactly
What it is a rare case. David taylor
Wrote about one of these cases
in his book entitled my trip to heaven.

Held Captive By Religion.

In His book david Says
that menTal illness is a
difficult disease to heal.
He also said we do not see
many healings of this kind.

IF you are reading this
book. And you are suffering from
a mental illness. Or maybe a
family member you know is.
The best thing you can do is,
to get them the help they need.
I also Suffer from a mental illness
but i Am being treated for it.

Chapter Twelve

Freedom In Christ

There is a freedom that
We have in christ. It is
a freedom to make mistakes
and learn from them. A freedom
to express ourself and our
Christan beliefs. As well as
Our Viewpoints about life.

Every Christan makes
mistakes, but not every
Christan learns from them.
It's good to express yourself
in a manner that brings Joy
to you and your family.

Some people express themselves
With cool Hairstyles or with
expensive clothes and Jewelry.
There is nothing wrong with
that. If you are giving god the
first 10 percent of your income
you deserve to be happy and express
yourself if any way you feel.

It's only when we become
Selfrighteous that we look
to conform our image into
what we believe is biblically
correct. It is your heart and
mind that needs to be conformed
into the image of ChrisT. The
clothes you wear don't make
or break you.

Now when it comes to a young
women dressed scandalously
it is dangerous. Only because
it brings unwanted attention
to that person. There are a lot
of Christans that
have a good Heart but the way
they dress and would seem to
Suggest other wise.

There are also Christan men
and women Who go places, that
are considered controversial.
They go to places such
as bars clubs and casinos

When i was young christan
I would go to the bar sometimes
and to clubs. When i
Would go out it would be to
Socialize.

The more i look back on those
days. I do think i would have
been better off finding a
better place to socialize. The
reason i say that is because sheep
and wolves Just donT mix.

I do wish christans would
rise up and create fun places
to hangout at, without all the
Worldly vices we see prevalent
in today's Society.

I can't wait for the millennial
reign to begin. That will be
fun let me tell you!!

When i was teaching on youtube.
I came a crossed a christan
Hip Hop Artist named go tracks.
Go tracks was given a vision
from the lord. He was Shown
People In heaven playing football.
The coach even came up to him
and asked him Would he like to
Run some play's. Go track was
also showed, what look like a
Valley or a split in the earth.
Where he saw what looked to be clubs
where christan would go to dance.

With there friends. There
was even a Dj!!

Another prophet was shown
The millenial reign. He goes
by the name elvi zapata. he
he saw a man that
liked to play golf. In this mans
backyard was a Whole gulf
Course. given to him by Jesus
himself

Also he also saw
Other people having fun. Enjoying
activities like fishing boating
and camping. The millenial reign
will be full of awesome activities
that us christians can utilize
for recreational purposes.

Brother zappita also seen
an rv in heaven. He was told
it was for him and his family
to use. So that they could
travel throughout the new
earth. He also saw a high
Speed train for travel purposes.

I personally had many visions
of both heaven and the new earth.
In one of my visions i saw
what looked to be a mall. It had
everything you could think of. and
Some things the human mind could not
even conceive of. I heard music
that sounded like hip hop but
Very angelic in nature.
I would watch as some of the
People would enter the mall and
immediately their song was played.
Also i never seen anyone pay
for anything you would just go
into the store and take
what you want. I seen two
of my friends that have passed
away walking around this place.
It was very beautiful.

Heaven is not going to be
Some place where we sit around
and play harps all day. We will
not worship God 24/7. There
is laughter Joy and fun. I see
exciting times right ahead of
us.

Do you enjoy doing some of the
things you have read about today?
Would you like to do them
in eternity? Pray this prayer
with me and you can be sure when
you die. These awesome
experiences will Await you.

Dear lord i confess that i
have not lived a life Worthy
of your KingDom. nor do i have
the ability to. But i Do believe
you can save me. Lord today i
put my trust in you. Guide me
Strengthen me. I pray these
things and more in Jesus
name amen.

In Conclusion

Good people sometimes do
bad things because of their
pride and lack of knowledge. Other
Times it is because they are
mentally unstable and they
do not have a good supporT
system. Prophecies will come
and go With time but the message
behind the prophecies will
always remain the same. repent
and be saved. The future for
Christans world wide is a bright
One. If they will Just answer
the call On their lives. Religion
can become a stumbling block if
we dont have a personal Relation
ship with the Lord. There is
Coming a time when God will
rule the earth with Peace, Love
and Justice will fill the
Land. and the world will never
be the Same. May the knowledge
and widom you read in this
book change your life
and cause you to prosper in
the land

Back Cover

This book is ment to
equipt prophets and pastors
with the knowledge and
wisdom to Avoid the pitt
falls many clergy make.
Also to give insight on Suicide
and the mental health of
belevers across the world.
This book also gives us
a look in the future of
America and the war's and rumors
of war we as a nation face.
And shows us what we have
to look forward to in the
1000 year
millennial reign with
God on earth.

Edward T McDonald is an
evangalist in the city
of Pittsburgh PA.

Edward is A born again beliver
And enjoys spending
his time ministering
throughout the city